HOW TO
BRAIN
TRAIN
YOUR CAT

HOW TO BRAIN TRAIN YOUR CAT

An exclusive edition for

for all your gift books and gift stationery

This edition first published in Great Britain in 2020 by
Allsorted Ltd, Watford, Herts, UK WD19 4BG

© Susanna Geoghegan Gift Publishing

Author: Helen Redding

Images used under license from Shutterstock.com

Cover design: Milestone Creative

Contents design: Jo Ross, Double Fish Design Ltd

ISBN: 978-1-91229513-5

Printed in India

10 9 8 7 6 5 4 3 2 1

HOW TO
BRAIN
TRAIN
YOUR
CAT

Contents

LET THE GAMES COMMENCE!

DEALING WITH SPECIFIC PROBLEMS

TAKING IT TO THE NEXT LEVEL

BRAIN TRAINING NOTES

Time spent with cats is never wasted.

SIGMUND FREUD

INTRODUCTION

Brain training involves games and puzzles that can stop your brain from stagnating, and keep you young forever (well, maybe not forever). Its benefits are recognised, and people are starting to realise the value that brain training can potentially have for our pets. No, it is not a fad – it is a real thing! In the way that we can do crosswords, sudokus and logic puzzles to keep our brains stimulated, your cat can reap enormous benefits from similar brain exercises. Although they obviously can't hold a pen ...

You play with your cat and send them out to go who-knows-where to get their physical exercise – there's absolutely no reason why you shouldn't start exercising their brain, too. We know what you're thinking: "My cat? I can train it? Will it actually deign to listen to me without giving me that look and stalking off?" Yes. Well, there are no guarantees, but what's for certain is you've got nothing to lose and lots to gain. Give it a go and most of all have fun – together.

In this book, we'll explain how brain training works, and give you practical tips and ideas to share with your cat. You'll discover how enjoyable brain training can be as a way to interact and bond with your feline best friend.

Cats will outsmart dogs every time.

JOHN GROGAN

UNDERSTANDING HOW YOUR CAT'S BRAIN WORKS

WHAT IS
BRAIN
TRAINING?

Are you imagining a brain wearing a sweatband, Lycra and doing squats? You wouldn't be far off. Also known as cognitive training, brain training uses mental exercises to flex and hone your cognitive skills in the same way you'd tone your muscles in the gym. Brains can be trained to be smarter, fitter, faster and more responsive. But you do have to put the work in.

The skills normally targeted by brain training are:

- long- and short-term memory
- logic and reasoning
- sensory processing
- attention.

If you're a cat owner wanting the best for their wellbeing, then the good news is that brain training isn't just for humans.

Okay, so your cat might not be as compliant as a human when it comes to asking them to do something, but their brains are surprisingly similar to ours. Of course, your cat would argue that their brain is far superior!

This book will show you how to use the techniques of brain training to work with your cat and keep their brains in tip top condition. It will help you to understand how your cat interacts with – and interprets – the world, and how you can work together to get the best out of each other. The more you understand how your cat functions, the better you will be able to cater for their needs and live harmoniously (to the extent that a cat will let you!).

Most importantly, you'll find out how to keep brain training with your cat fun. If it stops being fun, don't do it. Stress is completely counterproductive to learning and wellbeing. As a pet owner, your job is to be responsible and keep your cat safe, secure, happy and healthy, so focus on making brain training an enjoyable and beneficial part of everyday life.

DOES YOUR CAT NEED
BRAIN
TRAINING?

Even though your cat likes to give the impression that they're self-sufficient – dare we say aloof? – they do still need plenty of interaction and attention to keep them healthy and happy. And that means stimulating them mentally, as well as encouraging physical exercise and cat-like behaviour such as climbing and hunting.

If you're concerned that your cat's brain isn't active enough, there are certain warning behaviours to look out for that could suggest they're bored:

- excessive grooming and shedding

- scratching furniture

- sleeping (even) more than usual

- being aggressive towards other pets

- weeing and pooing where they shouldn't be, e.g. outside of the litter box

- disinterest, or, at the other end of the spectrum, excessive interest in food.

If your cat is experiencing any of the above and there are no medical reasons for the behaviour, you need to do a brain stimulation audit right away! Think about yourself for a moment: how would you feel if your senses and brain were being deprived? For humans, there are many negative side effects to long-term sensory deprivation, including extreme anxiety and depression, and the same effects can be seen in pets.

Cats are slightly trickier to deal with than, say, dogs. You probably don't take your cat for long walks in the park, throwing sticks for endless games of fetch and therefore ticking off those boxes. Your cat takes itself out to roam, jump and climb and get much of the physical exercise it needs to stay healthy. When it comes to playing with your cat – and brain training – it's likely to be an indoors-based pursuit, and the attention parametres will be very different to that of an eager-to-please dog. Be patient, and remember the benefits of stimulating your cat's brain!

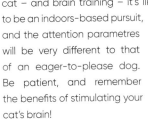

CAN ANY CAT BE BRAIN TRAINED?

When you look at your cat, you get a knowing look back: the look that says "I know more than you" and "What could you possibly teach me, human?". Can brain training work at all, or will it simply be a battle of wills that your cat inevitably wins ... again?

Cats all have different personalities, and you'll know your own cat well – what they like and dislike, and what they do and don't respond to. Brain training won't work perfectly with every cat, just as we as humans click with some ways of learning but are totally bamboozled by others. Some cats will be harder to work with, for example those that struggle interacting with humans or that are suffering the aches and pains of old age or long-term illness. On the other hand, some cats will pick brain training up easily, and start teaching you a thing or two (like they always knew they could).

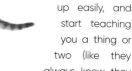

It's often assumed that cats can't be trained, but this isn't true. Cats are highly intelligent creatures, and can easily be taught a variety of behaviours – fundamental when you don't want them to be weeing on your carpet. Kittens are much easier to train than adult cats, and are better at adapting. Although adult cats are still able to adapt to new things – new experiences, people, homes – kittens can do it almost automatically.

However, don't let your cat's age deter you from trying brain training. Cats' brains are very similar to ours – soft and pliable, adapting to new information and capable of changing habits given the right stimulation. Yes, it gets harder in the advancing years – that's why we have the phrases "You can't teach an old dog new tricks" and "Set in your ways". But mental stimulation should be an everyday part of your pet's life, whatever their age, just as physical exercise is.

Cats are brilliant at being cats. They can sleep most of the day and then still muster up the energy to catch a mouse or frog to bring home to you as a gift. It's great being a cat. Most of the cats that people have as pets are a mixture of breeds, so whether some breeds of cats are smarter than others is a tricky question.

Like with dogs, when rating the intelligence of a cat, we tend to think about how interested the cat is in doing what we want it to and interacting with us. Those breeds that are better at interacting with humans are those that are athletic and well-known for being nosey – Siamese and Burmese cats, along with the Bengal. Heavier, larger cats such as Persians and Himalayans aren't so fussed about being active with you, and are therefore considered to be less intelligent. That's unfair on them, and probably not the case at all. Anyway, who cares how clever you are if you get to sleep 20 hours a day?

HOW IS YOUR CAT'S
BRAIN
WIRED?

To understand how brain training works, you need to understand your cat's brain. What makes cats tick and how are they different to other animals, including us?

Cats can be difficult to study in scientific experiments because compared to dogs, for example, they are notoriously uncooperative and can get stressed very quickly. (So no, dogs aren't cleverer than cats – it's just that the "intelligence" tests for dogs don't transfer to felines.) As a result, we have very little knowledge about cats – just how they'd like it to stay! However, research places a cat's intelligence alongside that of a 2-year-old toddler – the same as a dog's level of cognition. This is demonstrated by the following workings of a cat's brain:

- Object permanence: Cats have the ability to keep an object in mind even when it is out of sight. For example, if you show them one of their toys and then hide it under a cushion, they'll know it's under the cushion rather than assuming it's vanished into thin air.

- Physical causality: Cats understand physical cause and effect. For example, if a cat is presented with several lengths of string, only one of which has food attached to it, the cat knows to pull the string with the food on it.

- Quantities: It would be a stretch to say that cats can actually count (see page 78), but research does show that cats can discriminate between quantities. For example, when offered different quantities of food in different numerical combinations, they are more likely to choose the larger quantities.

Cats have a great short-term memory – they can remember things for about 16 hours. Compare that to a dog's short-term memory of 5 minutes! No wonder dogs chase their tails. Not much is known about the long-term memory of cats; however, given that their cerebral cortex is complex, we can assume that their long-term memory is relatively good.

Sadly, like humans, as cats age their brain can deteriorate. Feline cognitive dysfunction syndrome is very much like Alzheimer's disease and can lead to depression, confusion and anti-social behaviour. In 2015, Alzheimer's Society in the UK funded research to test whether brain training games can improve the cognitive function of people over 60. The study found that over 6 months, brain training helped people to get on better with their daily activities. Another good reason to give it a try with your cat.

Cats have a great ability to learn new information, connect it with other information, remember it and then utilise that knowledge in other situations. Thanks to the feline disregard for cooperating with scientists, we may never know the full range and depth of what cats' brains are capable of!

FELINE
SENSES

Understanding how your cat's senses function is important for appreciating exactly how they play and learn. Humans are far more advanced at processing information and thoughts thanks to our highly developed prefrontal cortex, but we know that cats aren't that far behind. And when it comes to senses, they exceed our abilities.

SIGHT

Cats don't see in as much detail as we do. In fact, your face will look blurry to your cat until you're about 2–3 feet away. We also see colours much better than they do. They can distinguish between blues and greens but struggle with reds.

Yet your cat's eyes are brilliant in other respects. They only need about a sixth of the light that we need to see – they can't see in the dark, but it does make them awesome hunters in near darkness.

Cats also have a special reflective layer at the back of the eyeball, which reflects light back onto the retina and makes their vision in low light even better. (It's this special layer that makes cats' eyes glow spookily in the dark.) The pupil shape in a cat's eye is also very different to a human's, and can open and close much more rapidly to adjust to light.

HEARING

Cats have amazing hearing. They can hear frequencies of up to 60kHz – humans can only hear up to around 20kHz (dogs 45kHz). To give an example of your cat's incredible ears: they hear the high-pitched squeak of a mouse before they even see it. Using their hearing alone, they can detect their prey accurately – combine that with their wonderful vibration-detecting whiskers and they're a predator to be reckoned with.

This all means that the world can be pretty noisy for your cat. Much of their experience takes place in the higher end of the auditory spectrum, so they respond well to high-pitched sounds. Try calling them sounding like you've sucked the air from a helium balloon and then like you're Barry White – you'll notice a difference in the way they respond!

Even when they appear to be chilling, your cat's ears will be subtly moving and staying alert to danger. Did you know that cats can turn their ears independently and through 180 degrees? To manage this, cats have 30 muscles for moving their ears. Compare that to the 6 muscles we have, and you'll understand why humans find it so tricky to even wiggle their ears a little!

SMELL

Smell is one of your cat's most important senses. Cats are born blind and deaf, so from day 1 their nose is of vital importance, for example for locating their mother's milk. They have 200 million smell receptors – compare that to the 5–6 million that humans have, and you'll see how feeble our sense of smell is!

THE FLEHMEN REACTION

While it might sound like an Oscar-winning film, the Flehmen reaction is a response shared by many animals – cats curl back their upper lip and inhale through their nostrils, sensing something (often with no detectable odour). Picking up particles with their tongue, the particles get passed into their mouth and on to their vomeronasal organ (or Jacobson's organ) on the roof of their mouth. It enables your cat to combine taste and smell. It's a remarkable ability that lets cats learn information about their environment, particularly about other (eligible!) cats that might be around. You're likely to see your cat do it after you've opened the door for them to go outside.

TASTE

Let's just say that it's a good job cats have a great sense of smell! When it comes to taste, cats only have 473 taste buds – compare that to the human tongue with its 9,000 taste buds. Smell rather than taste is more likely to determine what your cat eats. If it smells good, your cat will eat it.

WHY DOES YOUR
CAT
LIKE PLAYING?

Brain training is all about playing games. Despite looking like they'd be happy sleeping pretty much 24/7 (perhaps deigning to get up for some food), cats do like to play. Okay, so you're unlikely to ever see the excitement in a cat's face that you do a dog's when you pick up a toy. Nonetheless, play – and the stimulation and time with you it brings – is an important part of your cat's life.

For cats, play has several functions:

- In the wild, playing helps kittens to learn vital survival skills like stalking, batting, pouncing and catching prey. This predatory instinct stays strong in domesticated cats, and play becomes a natural outlet for it.

- It helps build social relationships, not just with other cats but with humans, too. (They do love you even though they don't always show it, really they do.)

- Energetic play can help combat weight problems, especially if your cat is an indoor cat that doesn't get the chance to climb fences or trees or flee your angry neighbour after digging up a flower bed.

How much time should you spend playing with your cat? A few short sessions of around 5 minutes every day should be enough for your cat to reap the benefits. It's not just your cat who will enjoy playing – owners deserve some playtime and a stress-releasing wellbeing boost too! You'll know your cat well enough to know when they've had enough and it's time for you back off.

If you can make brain training part of everyday life with your cat, it will help avoid any annoying or destructive attention-seeking behaviour that may develop if your moggy is bored and unstimulated. Is your cat reluctant to play? Have a look at *Encouraging playing* on page 48 for some tips to get them going.

HOW DO
CATS
LEARN?

What makes your cat tick? We've seen in *Feline senses* (page 18) how they use their sight, hearing and smell to understand the world around them. We also know that their natural instincts dictate a lot of their behaviour, even though domesticated cats have become well accustomed to monopolising our comfy chairs and being pampered to high heaven.

How does your cat learn? Your clever cat picks things up in lots of different ways. One such way is through association, and this forms an important part of making brain training work (see *Positive reinforcement*, page 30). For example, your cat will learn that dinner is on the way when they hear you open up their food – and there they'll be, right under your feet. Association and habit come arm in arm, so a regular occurrence such as dinnertime becomes ingrained quickly in your cat's brain.

Cats are incredibly fast learners. Beware that anything you inadvertently teach them – such as chasing your toes under the bedsheets – will fast become expected by your cat, and you'll soon realise how annoying and unwelcome such behaviour is. The phrase is "making a rod for your own back". You've been warned …

Cats also learn a huge amount from observing things (which really makes you wonder what's going through their mind when they're trying to stare you out). Not only do they learn from observing their environment, but they also learn from watching other kittens/cats and, of course, us. Plus, although they'd like to believe they're infallible, cats learn from trial and error just as we do. Skidding off a slippery worktop and hitting the floor is something a cat will only do once!

As a cat owner, you have the power to help your cat learn that certain situations don't need to be stressful. For example, if your cat despises being crated up for trips to the vet, then you can use positive associations to ease the stress of the experience. If your cat associates going into their crate with receiving cuddles and tasty treats, they're more likely to stay calm and cooperate. And remember how they learn from your behaviour – if you're getting worked up and anxious, your cat will pick up on that, and it will impact their own behaviour. Be mindful!

Training dogs relies on their unique sensitivity to human body language and their innate affection for whoever looks after them. Dogs are also fundamentally sociable, reflecting their origins as wolves living in family groups. Cats, however, are descended from solitary territorial animals, and are generally wary of social contact. Yet this profound difference in the way cats see us compared with how dogs should not obscure the fact that these two creatures learn, for all intents and purposes, in the same way. It's their motivations for learning that differ.

THE BENEFITS OF BRAIN
TRAINING:
YOUR CAT

Cats don't give without expecting something back. (Not to imply that they're selfish!) And neither would you embark on brain training without expecting it to benefit your cat and you. Aside from it being lots of fun, there are plenty of reasons for giving it a go that have fantastic health boosts for your cat. You just need to keep plenty of patience on hand!

WHAT WILL MY CAT GAIN?

We expect our cat to fit in with our human world, but for most cats, it can be a stressful place. Lots of noise, humans looming over them, children chasing them, other cats and even the odd pesky dog to contend with. We trap them inside for long periods when most cats just want to be out catching birds, chasing butterflies and pooing in the neighbour's garden. Brain training can help your cat deal with the demands that we and our home environment place on them.

Your cat's priority is a secure place to live with a source of food. When they encounter something unfamiliar – and potentially scary – your cat's first reaction is to run away and hide somewhere safe. This makes it incredibly hard for a cat to learn how to handle situations they feel nervous in – they're not good at "feeling the fear and doing it anyway". Along with creating a comfortable and safe home environment, brain training is one way of helping your cat better adapt to stressful situations.

How else is brain training good for your cat? Here are the main benefits:

- It encourages natural behaviours (e.g. jumping, stalking, batting) that promote both physical and mental wellbeing, and reduces the chance of troublesome behavioural issues.

- It exposes your cat to new things to increase mental stimulation, resulting in a happier, more engaged life – rather than just sitting in a cardboard box all day on top of the hot water pipe running under the kitchen floor ...

- It increases your cat's overall levels of physical activity. Don't worry, they'll still get their HOURS of sleep.

- It raises their heart rate, just like we aim for at the gym.

- It stops boredom. Chilled as they may seem, your cat still needs to keep its brain active to avoid stress and frustration. Have you ever seen a photo of a 4,000-year-old mummified Egyptian cat? That's exactly the opposite of what you're aiming for.

AND WHAT WILL THEY LOSE?

Cats will lose nothing apart from any undesirable behaviour that stems from lack of stimulation and boredom. Will they lose their aloofness? No, of course not! If they lost that, they wouldn't be a cat. There is so much to gain from brain training even if you only manage to get your cat interested in a few simple games. It takes work and patience, but it's well worth the effort. Just don't expect your cat to do anything other than walk away from you with its tail in the air, butt on display, at the end of it all.

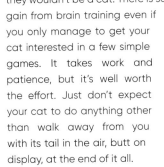

THE BENEFITS OF BRAIN
TRAINING:
YOU

Even though cats are solitary animals and often look at you as if to say "impress me, human", owning a cat is still a relationship. You dedicate an awful lot of time to keeping your cat happy. You provide the security they need, a reliable source of food and, of course, comfy chairs and carpet to scratch. The love and affection that your cat (regularly/sometimes/very occasionally* – *delete as appropriate) returns to you makes it all worthwhile. Hopefully, brain training will reap rewards for you, too.

While spending time playing brain games with your cat, you – as an owner – are being trained just as much as they are. What can you learn?

- How to interpret your cat's body language and behaviour.

- How to communicate more effectively with your cat.

- How best to speak to and interact with your cat to get the response you want.

- Positive reinforcement is a huge part of any training, including brain training. Learn how it works and how to use it to get the best behaviour from your cat (see page 30).

You'll find these useful skills for being a cat owner generally, not just for brain training. As cats are independent souls, it's tempting to just let them get on with it. However, you cannot expect your cat – especially if it's a kitten – to learn things by itself, even if natural instincts do play a big part in their life. Some training is essential, for example using the litter tray rather than pooing on your expensive rug, but any extra training you can do will make life with your cat a whole lot easier.

We all know how cats like to be king or queen of the jungle, but don't let that stop you setting rules and boundaries. In fact, that's exactly why you should! If you don't want your cat sniffing around on the worktop (with paws fresh from the litter tray) then teach them not to. Your cat needs to feel safe and secure, so give them this structure and routine. Without these in place, your cat will become ruler of all they survey – and that includes you. So make life easy on yourself and get your cat following at least some of your rules.

POSITIVE
REINFORCEMENT

Don't be fooled by your cat's calm exterior. They know how to push your buttons. Whether it's scratching your furniture or climbing the curtains, every cat has the potential for naughtiness and bad behaviour. It's how you react that's important if you want to make sure that giving your cat a telling off doesn't leave them scared and confused – or leave you upset and frustrated.

Positive reinforcement is simple; it means rewarding good behaviour. Now comes the tricky bit to accept – it also means ignoring bad behaviour. (Not so different from how some experts believe you should treat children.) It works on the principle that we prefer to be praised rather than punished. So, it's more effective to teach your cat what they should do than try to teach them what they shouldn't. By rewarding the desirable behaviour, your cat is more likely to repeat that behaviour. Positive reinforcement is therefore an incredibly powerful tool for training your cat.

The reward (see *Treats and rewards*, page 43) needs to come within seconds of the good behaviour or else your cat will have no idea why they're being rewarded and won't associate the two. If you reward your cat two minutes after using their scratching post when they've climbed into their basket – guess what? They'll think you're praising them for sitting in their basket. Timing is crucial, and so is consistency. Consistency is one of the most important things to focus on when training any pet. Everyone in the house should know how positive reinforcement works and which behaviours they need to reward the cat for. A lack of consistency will leave your cat dazed and confused.

Remember that "bad" behaviour can be caused by a failure to meet your cat's needs. Cats don't act out of malice or spite – it's more likely to be stress and anxiety. Look at what's causing the unwanted behaviour, and make the necessary changes. If it's something in the home environment that's making your cat feel insecure, then increase their comfort by fixing it. As this book has already said, brain training can play a big part in reducing the stress that cats experience due to boredom. Combine it with positive reinforcement, and you can quickly put a stop to undesirable behaviour. And, most importantly, you'll have a happy cat.

BUILDING A
STRONG
BOND

Your bond with your cat forms the basis of your whole relationship. If your cat isn't a natural snuggler, it may feel like you're having to work hard to build that bond with them. Even when you think you've bonded, your cat will have ways of reminding you that you're only 5% there! That nip on the hand, that swipe round the face – they'll let you know who really has the upper hand in your relationship. But don't be put off. Building a bond with your cat provides the all-important security they need to feel content.

Try these top tips for happy bonding:

1. Space. Whether you're bringing home a kitten or an adult cat, it is incredibly important to give them space. Take it slowly

and resist lavishing them with love and cuddles. Give them a chance to process what's going on, and make sure they have somewhere to hide to gather their thoughts. It's about respecting them.

2. Be consistent. If your cat knows what to expect of you and of their routine, they will trust you.

3. Become a positive association yourself! Your cat needs to associate you with good things happening. For example, have

a treat in your pocket ready for when your cat does something that deserves praise.

4. Cats love to groom themselves, and to be groomed by you. Pick a time for grooming when your cat is relaxed and content. They prefer regular, rhythmical strokes as they don't like surprises! Along with encouraging bonding, grooming is a great way for both you and your cat to relieve stress.

5. Patience is so important when building a bond with your cat. It's highly unlikely that you'll become best buddies on first sight, but invest time in your cat and you'll be rewarded with positive results.

Spending time brain training your cat is a fantastic way to create a bond with them. To make it successful and fun, it's important to keep in mind all of the suggestions above. You'll then be on the right path to making brain training fun and beneficial.

If your cat is bonding with you, you'll start to see certain bonding behaviours:

- Kneading. Think of this as a mini-massage – often with claws out, so be prepared for a little bit of ouchiness on occasions. If an adult cat kneads you with their paws, it means they're feeling relaxed and comfortable around you – it's a great sign that you're doing something right.

- Bunting. This is when your cat walks up to you and rubs you with their forehead. Bunting can be accompanied by other friendly behaviours like purring and sitting on your lap.

I have studied many philosophers and many cats. The wisdom of cats is infinitely superior.

HIPPOLYTE TAINE

CAT FACTS
HOW TO SPOT IF YOUR CAT IS DEPRESSED

If your cat isn't being sufficiently stimulated physically and mentally, and isn't getting enough interaction with you, it can lead to depression. Are they behaving differently to normal? Here's what to look out for:

1. Over eating, under eating or not eating at all. A definite sign that something is amiss.

2. Vocal cues. Is your cat talking less than usual? Or has your normally quiet cat started to make lots more noise? Low, mournful sounding yowls can be a sign that your cat is feeling sad and miserable.

3. Under or over grooming.

4. Hiding or very clingy behaviour. Your cat might also lose interest in activities that they normally get excited about, for example playing with a favourite toy.

5. Aggressive behaviour. Is your cat normally friendly and relaxed? If your cat is feeling unhappy, it is often expressed through aggression or fear.

6. Changes in toilet habits and spraying. Watch out for your cat urinating in inappropriate places outside of their litter tray. They could be using their scent to make themselves feel better.

7. Scratching. Is your cat scratching things more than usual, trying to mark their territory?

8. Sleeping when they would normally be awake.

If your cat is displaying any of these signs, you should also get them checked out by your vet to rule out any underlying medical conditions.

Cats are a mysterious kind of folk. There is more passing in their minds than we are aware of.

SIR WALTER SCOTT

GETTING
STARTED

WHAT
DO YOU
NEED?

To set out on your brain training adventure with your cat, you don't need much more than a knapsack full of treats, and patience. If you want to spice things up and add a bit of variety, it's worth investing in a few items to keep your cat interested. So, what props and toys do you need to make brain training as effective, fun and easy as possible?

Getting together some fun toys doesn't need to be expensive, or indeed cost anything at all. If you've owned cats before, you'll know their obsession with squeezing themselves into a cardboard box even if it's far too small for them. An empty box just has to appear for 30 seconds for your cat to make it its home – it gives your cat a great feeling of security. Have a look around your home for other items you can use for games:

- Stuff an old sock with crinkly wrapping paper and tie a knot at the open end of the sock. Instant prey!

- Two ping pong balls in a bowl of water – great for batting as well as encouraging your cat to drink more.

- The classic toilet roll! Simple. There's nothing cats love scratching more than cardboard (apart from your carpet).

- Cut holes in the top of a Tupperware container (being careful not to leave any sharp edges) or a box. Put some toys or treats inside and watch your cat puzzle how to extract the contents through the holes.

- Good old paper cups are ideal for hiding treats under.

- Recycle your old clothes. A strip of old t-shirt tied in a knot makes a great toy for chasing, pouncing on and generally attacking. Tie it to a piece of string and attach the string to a stick and you'll have the perfect cat wand – and it'll be plastic-free unlike many you buy in the shops.

If you really want to pamper your puss, there are of course plenty of cat "intelligence" toys on the market – ranging from the simple to the fancy – that can help with brain games:

- Cat puzzles. No, these aren't jigsaws – that would be tricky even for a polydactyl cat! Think more along the lines of puzzles with holes and sliding components that encourage your cat to figure out how to get out what's inside (toys, treats).

- Treat dispensers and food mazes. Make your cat work for their food, and get their brain ticking louder than their rumbling tummy.

- Self-massage centres. Yes, they're a thing. And a thing most humans would love, too.

- If you're planning on trying clicker training then – you've guessed it – you'll need to buy a clicker.

- You'll also find lots of activity toys that you can pop a battery in to replace human exertion, for example feathers on a stick that spin randomly.

With all toys – whether homemade or shop bought – if you spot any damage or small pieces coming off, take the toy away from your cat as it could pose a danger to them. Always supervise playtime and brain training to ensure your cat is safe and well.

TREATS
AND
REWARDS

Food is a fantastic motivation for training any animal, and cats are no exception. Compared to dogs, cats can be less responsive to the promise of treats. In the wild, cats hunt small prey and don't exert huge amounts of energy hunting (and conserve a lot by sleeping most of the day). What this means is that cats have learnt not to expend more energy than their food supplies. Why would they therefore spend 10 minutes leaping around for you in return for a tiny piece of kibble? For cats, that simply doesn't add up!

When using treats with brain training, the key rule is that the treats are there to positively reinforce behaviour rather than for bribery. Rewards should come at the moment an action has been completed to create that positive association for your cat. They shouldn't be used like a carrot on a stick, for example to encourage your cat through an activity. Keep the treats out of sight until it's time to lavish your cat with praise and say "well done".

What makes a good brain training treat?

- Must be easy to carry around and give to your cat. Bear in mind you're likely to have pockets full of treats for weeks.

- Must be quick to eat and easily swallowed or you'll spend valuable training time waiting for your cat to finish munching.

- Must be irresistible and completely delicious in order for your cat to think it's worth the effort. Make the treats more appealing than your cat's usual kibble or they'll simply give you that bored look.

Will your cat get overweight with all these extra goodies? No,

as long as you're giving them lots of opportunities for physical exercise and only use reward-based training short-term. Avoid any treats that exceed 10% of your cat's recommended total daily calorie intake. Also, avoid over-rewarding your cat – too much of a good thing can be boring. As soon as your cat has made the necessary positive associations and is responding well to you, you can reduce the frequency and quantity of treats they get, and make it more random. Your cat won't unlearn what they've mastered – the positive associations will stick – but do keep practicing and replace treats with a rewarding scratch in your cat's favourite spot.

Here are some ideas for kitty treats:

- Your cat's normal dry food. They're guaranteed to like it, but see boredom caution above!

- Shop-bought dry or semi-dry treats. Usually fairly low-calorie (do double check though) and more easily palatable than standard cat food. Try some flavours that your cat doesn't usually get to experience in their everyday food.

- Small chunks of cooked meat (although watch out for delicate tummies if your cat isn't used to it, and only use in moderation).

WORD OF WARNING: Avoid any foods that are toxic to cats – for example, raisins, grapes, chocolate, onions, alcohol, salt, tea, coffee, raw fish, etc.

And a final word on treats – don't use them to replace love! A handful of treats might be convenient, but they will never create the same kind of bond between you and your cat as strokes, cuddles and grooming.

FITTING
BRAIN
TRAINING
IN TO YOUR DAY

Making brain training a regular feature of your day isn't as hard as it might sound. Playing with your cat is an important part of their routine, and brain training is simply another form of play. You're not embarking on anything above and beyond what you'd be doing anyway. You're just giving it more structure, variety and hopefully more focused results ... and making it even more fun.

Try to set aside some time each day. You're the best judge of your cat's personality and tolerance levels, so you'll know how much time they're likely to engage for. Five minutes a day might be all they can manage, but if your cat is enjoying it and you're seeing results, gradually build up the time and frequency. If one or both of you isn't in the mood when the time comes, don't force it – just try again another time. A frustrated owner trying to train an uninterested cat isn't going to work!

Remember, it's always best to end training on a high note. Be the one who calls an end to it before your cat stops enjoying themselves. That way, they'll associate brain training with positive feelings, and will be left wanting more.

If you can only squeeze a few minutes of brain training into your day, that's one hundred times better than no brain training at all. Experiment to see what works best for you and your cat – try different times of day but stick to the same location to give your cat the sense of security it needs. If you're using treats then you might find them more effective if your cat is hungry, so avoid times when your cat's belly is full and the only thing they're motivated to do is sleep.

ENCOURAGING
PLAYING

If your cat is in a playful mood, you will find brain training a lot easier. What you want is an excited toddler and not a sulky teenager moaning about what you're making them do while they text their friends how much they hate you! How can you encourage your cat to play and make the brain training experience as beneficial as possible?

Kittens love to play, particularly during the first 4 months of their lives. After that point, they'll start to settle down a little and find their own preferred levels of playfulness. Cats continue to play throughout their lives – how much depends entirely on the individual cat. If you have a kitten, you should embrace their love of play and encourage it as much as you can. Not only does this help to build a bond between you, but it sets up good habits for the rest of their life. The more confidence you can give your cat at a young age, the more likely they are to be happy to try new things with you.

Older cats may be restricted by age-related aches and pains, and certainly won't play with the same energy and intensity as kittens. Generally, they'll take longer to train than a younger cat too. This shouldn't put you off brain training though. Just work to accommodate your cat's physical abilities (for example, if their legs aren't what they were, don't play any games that involve jumping) and their energy levels.

You'll soon learn what your cat likes, but here are some tips for encouraging them to play without overwhelming them:

- Use rewards for when they engage in the brain games (see *Positive reinforcement*, page 30, and *Treats and rewards*, page 43).

- Don't play for too long – learn to judge when your cat is about to get bored, and before they do, end the playing on a high note.

- Cats often prefer a high-pitched tone of voice. Use that to get them to come to you and to get involved. Don't act out of character though or you risk scaring your cat!

- Don't pick your cat up and plonk them into the middle of a game to get them involved. They won't respond well. (Likewise, if your cat isn't cuddly, don't reward them with cuddles!)

- Most of all, be kind and be safe (see page 52).

So to encourage play, take it slowly and stay calm. Remember that cats can be like coiled springs – highly sensitive to the environment around them, the slightest surprise or threat could turn playtime into coaxing-cat-out-from-under-the-sofa time. Be considerate and respect your cat – good things come to those who wait!

CLICKER
TRAINING

Clicker training sounds like something you'd do with a show pony. Unfortunately, it's not that exciting, so put away your sequined jodhpurs for now. Clicker training is another valuable technique to slip into your cat training tool belt. Like conventional reward-based training, it's used to encourage actions and behaviours through creating positive associations in your cat's brain. But how does it work?

A clicker is a device that clicks when you press it. It is as simple as that, but can have impressive results when training a pet. When your cat is behaving how you want them to, the idea is to click the clicker and immediately reward your cat with a treat. At first, the clicking won't mean anything to them, but when you constantly repeat it, they'll become aware that the click signals a reward is on its way.

The next stage in the thought process is for your cat to wonder what they were doing when they heard the click that earned them the reward. If all goes as planned, your cat will quickly realise that good behaviour triggers a click, and a click triggers a treat. This in itself is a great piece of brain training. Your cat must figure out how the process works – perfect for honing their problem-solving skills.

Using a clicker requires you to be on the ball, so no snoozing. You'll need your lightning reflexes to click at the right moment, which requires you to pay close attention to your cat. The click needs to be at precisely the right moment to create an association between it and the behaviour you want to encourage. The moment your cat is doing what you want them to – CLICK! It does take some practice, but it's well worth sticking at it because the results can be brilliant.

As usual, a word of warning – don't assume that clicker training will work for your cat. For some cats, it literally doesn't click. If you find it's not for them, try not to get frustrated; instead simply ditch the clicker for a click-free reward-based method. Don't make your life difficult – or your cat's – by plugging away at something that isn't working.

BE KIND,
BE SAFE

Brain training shouldn't be a chore. It should be something you choose to do with your cat because you care about their wellbeing and want to spend some time having fun with them. They might occasionally scowl at you for bothering them, but your intentions are good. If at any point brain training stops being fun, take a step back and consider what's going wrong. It's vital to take that pause so that you don't continue anything that is bad for you or your cat.

How can you tell if your cat is unhappy? Your cat's body language is a reliable indicator of how they are feeling, so be aware. When your cat is feeling anxious and stressed, they will keep their body, head and tail low to the ground. You may notice their ears flitting around listening out for threats, or else they may flatten them against their head. What your cat is cleverly doing is making themselves as small as possible while they assess the danger. If you see your cat behaving like this while brain training, STOP. Give verbal and physical reassurance until their body returns to its usual neutral position.

If your cat is feeling angry or scared, rather than making themselves small, they'll make themselves appear as big as possible. You'll notice them stand rigid and tall, arch their backs and fluff up their fur. Their eyes will be wide, with pupils fully dilated. Again, this is a massive signal to back off and give them a chance to settle.

And how about a happy cat? How can you be reassured when things are going well and your cat is keen to engage? A happy cat is easy to recognise: it tends to make you think "I wish I was a cat!". Everything about a contented cat screams out the word "relaxed", so their whiskers will be relaxed and their tail still, ears pointed forwards. If their tail is up, it's a friendly signal, likewise if it's curled over their back. You'll get a dreamy wink if you're especially lucky!

Without sounding full of doom, brain training will rarely go as you expect. You and your cat will have good days and you'll have bad days. A cat is a cat – they won't always play ball by human standards, so be prepared for that. Watch your own body language; your cat will pick up if you're frustrated with them, and that will simply start a downward spiral. Never physically force your cat to do something – *showing* them is always the best approach. Most important of all, losing your temper and shouting at or punishing your cat is cruel. It won't achieve anything beneficial. and you risk ruining your relationship with your cat.

In *What do you need?* (page 40) you'll find out what to look for with your brain training toys. The main thing to remember is that if anything gets damaged or starts to disintegrate, it needs to be kept away from your cat so there's no danger of them swallowing pieces or cutting themselves. Just use your common sense and your cat will stay safe and well.

The cat could very well be man's best friend, but would never stoop to admitting it.

DOUG LARSON

CAT FACTS
10 AMAZING PHYSICAL FACTS ABOUT YOUR CAT

1. Using their tail for balance and their powerful back legs, cats can jump 6 times their own length.

2. When cats walk, they move both legs on one side and then both legs on the other side. The only other mammals to walk like this are camels, brown bears and giraffes.

3. A house cat can run faster than Usain Bolt, reaching speeds of up to 30 miles per hour.

4. A cat's claws all curve downward. This means they're brilliant at climbing trees, but they can't climb down head first – they have to back down.

5. A house cat's genome is 95.6% tiger!

6. Compared to any other mammal, cats have the largest eyes relative to their head size.

7. Female cats tend to be right-pawed. Male cats are more likely to be left-pawed.

8. Just like human fingerprints, cats have a unique pattern on their nose.

9. Thanks to their 'righting reflex' (which sadly buttered toast

does not have), cats have survived falls of over 20 metres. They use their eyes and the balance organs in the inner ear to provide the information about where they are so that they land on their feet.

10. Cats sleep 70% of their lives. Not a surprise to most cat owners, but still an amazing fact!

CAT TAILS
SUPER SMART BLUE

Blue lives in the California hills with his humans. He's made his name by being a super smart feline. According to his owner, Nancy Sayles, Blue can tell the time. He gets up for breakfast at precisely the same time each day, and then at 6 p.m., like clockwork, Blue strolls over to his bowl to wait for his dinner. Most likely it's his clever internal clock at work, the same internal clock that makes you wake at 7 a.m. on a weekend even if you've not set your alarm and don't need to go to work.

But not only that – Blue can also take the wooden security stick from his owner's sliding glass door and push the door open to get out by himself. His owner also believes he understands phrases like "let's go and feed the fish".

Clever cat or just well-trained? It's hard to tell whether Blue is actually extraordinary or just an ordinary moggy that's got the hang of a few tricks. Either way, he might give your own cat something to aspire to, so tell them about him!

The ideal of calm exists in a sitting cat.

JULES RENARD

LET THE GAMES
COMMENCE!

FIRST STEPS

– TOP TIPS

You've got inside the workings of your cat's brain, accumulated some toys and treats and now you're ready to take your first steps in brain training. This is the start of something exciting! No doubt you look more excited than your cat does, but inside they'll be brimming with anticipation too ... possibly. What's the best way to make a start?

- It's important to avoid too much distraction when you're starting out. Find a quiet room and one that your cat is familiar with. The more secure they feel, the more likely they are to join in.

- Start slowly and don't expect too much. Both you and your cat are learning at this stage, so keep the first session short. Begin with the simpler games to get your cat used to the idea of the kind of things you'll be doing.

- Be consistent. Your cat makes associations through repetition, so if you change the goalposts constantly, they'll have no idea what to expect. That doesn't make for a happy cat.

- Keep your tone of voice consistent with what your cat is used to. Change it or get too excitable and they'll wonder who on earth the stranger is in the room! Remember too that your cat will pick up on any impatience in your voice, so keep frustration firmly under wraps.

- It's important to end the first session on a positive note. Practice something simple that your cat has already got the hang of and bolster their confidence. That way you'll be able to finish up with a treat and lots of praise. Everything you can do to make positive associations in your cat's brain will encourage them to learn and enjoy it.

If at any point your cat is giving you the message that they're fed up and have had enough – STOP! There's nothing to be gained from continuing. Stop when the fun stops.

TARGET
TRAINING

Target training is a fun exercise to get started with. It also forms part of lots of other games, and so is a good basic technique to learn. Target training teaches your cat to touch a part of their body to an object (the "target"). Just imagine if your cat could ring a bell with its nose when it wanted to go in the garden. (Actually, maybe that bell would be ringing a little too often.)

BRAIN GAME: GET NOSEY

Aim of the game: This is the easiest way to start target training. In this game, your cat will simply learn to touch an object with its nose.

1. Find an object to use as the target. It could be your hand or favourite toy, for example.

2. Show the target to your cat, placing it about half an inch in

front of their nose. If they're not interested, try rubbing some their favourite food on it – guaranteed to get them to take notice!

3. When your cat gives their attention to the target – even better if they touch it straightaway – reward them with a treat and lots of praise (and click your clicker if you're clicker training).

4. Repeat step 3 if all's going well. Repeat several times if it's not going well ...

5. If you're lucky, your cat will click with this in your first session. Don't worry if they don't, as every cat is different. When they've got the basics and can consistently touch the target, you can start to phase out the treats.

Teaching your cat to touch a target also is a useful way of getting them to do something that they might normally find stressful. A great example of this is getting them into their carrier to take them to the vet. If you put the target in their carrier, your cat should follow your instruction to touch the target – therefore putting themselves in and reducing the need for you to chase around the house trying to catch them. The next game shows you how ...

DINNER
TIME

Your cat needs to eat, so mixing games and dinner time is an easy way to incorporate brain training into your day. We're not talking about exhausting your cat by hiding their food in an impossible-to-find, out-of-reach place. Simply by making dinner time more of a challenge – rather than literally handing it to them on a plate – you can stimulate your cat's brain cells. Slowing down dinner time also has health benefits for your cat, as it cuts down on guzzling and slows down digestion.

BRAIN GAME: WHERE IS DINNER?

Aim of the game: To engage your cat's sense of smell and fantastic hunting skills.

Do you put your cat's food in the same place every day? The answer is probably yes. And that's absolutely fine as cats love to feel secure and to know what's what. However, try mixing it up every few days. Rather than the usual spot, put your cat's food bowl somewhere else that's slightly trickier to find. Your cat will love hunting it down, and their senses will be stimulated. The tricky thing for you will be trying to hide the food without your cat seeing. Most cats appear at your side at the mere sound of you walking towards the kitchen!

BRAIN GAME: SCAVENGER HUNT

Aim of the game: To keep your cat on their toes with a hunt for food around the home – perfect for maintaining physical and mental wellbeing.

1. Rather than just hiding a whole bowl of food, split up your cat's food into small portions, or even individual pieces, and hide it around the house.

2. Put some in easy-to-spot places to give your cat an idea of the game – and that it's for fun rather than you trying to make life difficult for them!

3. When your cat gets the hang of it, you can start to hide the food in harder-to-spot places. Your cat's nose will really have

to start to work. (Don't worry that they won't find the food – your cat's nose is incredible! See *Feline senses*, page 18.)

Extra tips: Don't hide the food anywhere you don't want your cat to be, for example on a shelf of your finest vases. Be on hand in case your cat gets frustrated with the hunt and you need to help them out. Finally, remember where you've left food so that you can collect up any uneaten bits – you don't want your cat dining out on food past its sell-by date.

NOT JUST FOR
DOGS!

Forget the idea that cats can't be trained like dogs – it's a myth. Cats are more than capable of learning many of the tricks you'd normally associate with dogs. And they probably do it with more style and grace! Stay, sit, come – these are all useful commands for your cat to learn, not just for tricks but also to keep them safe. If your cat can obey the command to "stay", you may save them from one day dashing out of an open door into the path of a vehicle. Plus, learning anything new will of course keep your cat's brain stimulated. So, how can you teach your cat to be like a dog, just better?

BRAIN GAME: SIT!

Aim of the game: This one doesn't really need explaining, does it? To teach your cat to sit on command. Avoid pushing your cat's bottom to the floor – they need to learn the action on their own, and forcing them will only be met with annoyance.

1. Find a quiet time when your cat is relaxed (and hungry because you'll be using treats).

2. Get your cat's attention and tell them to "sit". Keep you tone of voice level and encouraging – there's no need to bark the command at them. As you say "sit", hold a treat above their eye level and over their head. Your cat will tip their head back to follow the treat, and by doing so, should need to sit down to keep their balance. Immediately as they sit, repeat the word "sit" and reward with a treat. (Okay, so you didn't exactly make them sit on this first attempt, but what you're doing is starting to make the association.)

3. The next step is ... you've guessed it ... repeat, repeat, repeat. You'll gradually cement your cat's association between the command, the action and the treat. Eventually, your cat will learn to sit simply with your word cue and your raised hand. No treats necessary. Clever cat!

BRAIN GAME: STAY!

Aim of the game: To teach your cat to stay in position on command, and until you tell them to move. This game works best if you've already taught your cat how to sit (see above).

1. Ask your cat to sit. Then make a movement – it could be as subtle as scratching your nose – and if your cat stays still, give them a treat.

2. Gradually start to make bigger movements as you say "stay" and again, if your cat stays still, reward them. They'll start to catch on to what's going on and realise that staying motionless is to their (and their stomach's) benefit.

3. When your cat has grasped the idea of the cue word and reward to "stay", you can start to extend the length of time you ask them to stay. Don't get frustrated if they move when you don't want them to – just get them back to a sitting position and start again. As with any brain game, it will take a bit of perseverance, so don't give up.

BRAIN GAME: GO FLAT!

Aim of the game: To make your cat look like a rug. No, to teach your cat to lie down on command.

There are a couple of ways to do this. One way is to wait until your cat lies down by itself – as it does, say "flat" and give your cat a reward as their chest touches the ground. If you do this every time they lie down, they will start to associate the cue word "flat" with the action and the treat. As your cat gets the hang of it, phase out the rewards (or at least make them random to keep some sense of expectation!), they will respond to the command alone.

The second method is very similar to teaching your cat to sit (see above). Rather than hold the treat above their head, hold it down to the floor in front of them so they move into a flat position to reach it. Eventually, you'll be able to lose the treats and your cat will simply follow your command and the lowered hand signal.

BRAIN GAME: FETCH!

Aim of the game: To teach your cat to retrieve an object. It's not just dogs that are good at this – cats are perfectly capable too. Your cat will be fetching your slippers in no time, providing they don't feel that it's beneath them. If your cat likes to bring you "gifts" such as mice and frogs, this is a good sign that not only do they love you but they're also skilled retrievers!

1. Before you get going, you need to decide which is the best object to use for fetch. It needs to be something your cat is interested in, so their favourite toy is a good option. Make sure it's something that's easy to carry though.

2. With a treat in your hand, get your cat's attention by calling their name, throw the toy and say "fetch". When your cat lets you take the toy, reward them with a treat. They'll start to recognise the word "fetch" and the promise of an edible goodie.

3. As you practice more – don't worry if it takes weeks – your cat will find it great fun to bring the toy straight to you without you having to collect it from them. Be patient, it will take time.

BRAIN GAME: ROLL OVER!

Aim of the game: To teach your cat to roll over. We're now moving into something trickier, but cats can still show dogs a thing or two. It's helpful if they can already follow the command to "go flat". This maneuver is also easier if it starts off with your cat lying on their side rather than on their tummy with their paws tucked under.

1. Hold a favourite treat above your cat's nose and move it over the top of them so that they follow it with their head. Lured by the treat, they should automatically roll over onto their other side. Introduce the words "roll over" as you move the treat.

2. Keep practicing this until it clicks with your cat what they're supposed to do. You'll then be able to tell them to roll over simply with the verbal command and moving your hand over their head without the treat.

LEARNING VOCABULARY:

A, B, C

Teaching vocabulary to your cat is a great brain boost. Cats self-teach vocabulary to some extent, but you can also work on it with them to keep them mentally challenged and stimulated. And there's another big benefit – the more you understand each other, the stronger your bond and the happier you'll both be.

Compared to dogs, there's very little research into how many words cats can learn. However, it's estimated that they can learn around 25 to 30 words. We know that the cleverest dogs can learn up to 250 words, and some exceptionally bright dogs can learn around 1,000. As cat lovers, we can only assume that cats are equally as brilliant, it's just that they don't show off about it as much as dogs do! When teaching new words, positive reinforcement and treats are the way to get results – much the same as with any training.

Cats find it much easier to learn and remember words that are attached to concrete objects, for example words like "bowl" or "treat". They find it harder to learn abstract concepts – any nicety you whisper in your cat's hairy ear will therefore be interpreted more for its tone than its meaning.

BRAIN GAME: CONVERSATION STARTERS

Aim of the game: To teach your cat a phrase that will be useful to you both. (You may have to suspend your disbelief a little with this game as it essentially teaches your cat to talk. Yes, really!)

1. Think of a phrase to teach. Something like "time for dinner" or "go into the garden". Keep it short and use it consistently.

2. Every time you say "time for dinner", make sure that you produce their food. Your cat needs to see some benefit from all this effort or they will lose interest! Try to do it at roughly the same time each day to create the necessary associations in your cat's brain (the reason for this will also make sense when you get to step 4).

3. Keep practicing the above for several days, and then it's time to test whether your cat has caught on …

4. Rather than feeding your cat at the time they're accustomed to, delay it by an hour. No surprises, but during that time your cat will meow at you an awful lot! At this point you need to listen very, very carefully – listen out for your cat's meows sounding like your phrase "time for dinner". Pay attention to the tone and the rhythm of the syllables. With any luck, they'll be mimicking you saying "time for dinner"! If you spot it, reward them immediately so they associate the noise they've made with a treat.

5. Next time your cat wants their dinner, they'll tell you rather than simply pestering you with noise!

BRAIN GAME: SAY MY NAME

Aim of the game: To teach your cat to respond to its name.

Does your cat always respond to their name? Are you sure? Think about whether they respond every time. The chances are that they don't, or that they're simply responding to a sound. Cats haven't been domesticated for as long as their ready-to-please canine counterparts have, so they don't feel the same need to please or respect their humans. Harsh but true. However, you can teach your cat to up their response rate.

1. As always, a hungry cat makes for a great time to train as they will be highly motivated by rewards. With treats to hand, call your cat's name. Make your tone gentle and coaxing, not harsh. It may take a few tries, but when they finally come to you, congratulate them with a treat.

2. Keep going with this until your cat consistently comes to you when you call their name. At this point, you can start to phase out the treats.

It's important that once your cat fully recognises its name you only use it with positive associations. For example, don't use it in anger or when you're telling your cat off. Equally, try not to use their name in stressful situations like when you're trying to coax them into their carrier for a visit to the vet. Keep it happy, and keep it positive!

CAT FACTS
YOUR CAT'S AMAZING VOICE

Cats are impressive communicators, and can produce around 100 different vocalisations, including a wide variety of mews and meows. It's helpful to be able to understand what your cat is telling you when you're training them – it's a two-way process after all. An analysis of the whole range of your cat's noises would require a book all of its own, so here's just a taster of what your cat is trying to say to you:

- Purring. This can mean both contentment and nervousness (purring is your cat's way of self-soothing). Read the purr in its context!

- Chattering. You're most likely to hear this when your cat spots a bird outside. It indicates excitement at the promise of prey.

- Hissing. Your cat feels threatened, and is prepped and ready to fight.

- Yowling. Long and mournful, a throaty yowl can indicate that your cat is feeling sad, worried or uncomfortable.

- Meows. Only reserved for humans! When no longer kittens, cats stop meowing to each other.

    o Mewing or a short meow: "Hello!"
    o Lots of meows: "Hello! I'm really excited to see you!"

o Mid-level pitch meow: "I want/need/beg you ..."

o Long meow: "I DEMAND that you ..."

o Long, low meow: "You've got this wrong, human!'"

o High-level pitch meow: "GET YOUR FOOT OFF MY TAIL!"

CAT TAILS

OSCAR THE
CARE HOME CAT

Rescue cat Oscar lives in a nursing home in Rhode Island in the US. He works in the dementia unit, providing his services as part of a pet therapy programme.

When Oscar does his daily round of the patients, he's been known to stop with individuals and stay with them, curled up. Those people he chose to stay with would often pass away a few hours later. After they have died, Oscar leaves the room, his job as a source of comfort complete. According to staff at the care home, Oscar isn't a particularly friendly cat normally, but he is strangely drawn to those in need.

It's often said that cats have a mysterious sixth sense (see page 114). Perhaps Oscar is proof of this.

CAN YOUR CAT
COUNT?

Can cats count? It seems dogs can, so why not cats? Your cat would argue that it's the superior creature after all. Research has shown that cats might have an abstract idea of numbers up to around 7. It's also claimed that mother cats can count as they notice when one of their kittens is missing – how true this is, no one is really sure because they could simply be recognising a scent missing from their litter.

Cats are notoriously bad at cooperating with research, so perhaps we'll never know the true extent of feline mathematics. However, you can try a brain game with your cat to cultivate their maths mojo. The game is based on studies from 2009 and 2016 that investigated cats' sense of quantities and their ability to judge "more" and "less". Not strictly counting, but interesting nonetheless. You can then reach your own conclusion about whether your cat can really count!

BRAIN GAME: MORE OR LESS?

Aim of the game: To discover whether your cat can distinguish between "more" and "less". (Your cat will need to be hungry to play this one!)

1. Place three bowls in a row, each with a different quantity of food in them. (They don't need to be massive portions so just divide up your cat's usual meal.)

2. Call your cat over (if they're a normal cat, they'll be under your feet anyway at the mere whiff of food) and let them see the bowls.

3. Which bowl does your cat go to and eat from?

According to research, when given a choice, cats tend to choose the bowl with the most food in it. Why? The main reason stems from cats' hunting instincts. In the wild, they would rather catch one big fat mouse than expend the effort to catch six skinny mice. Cats, lazy? Who said that?!

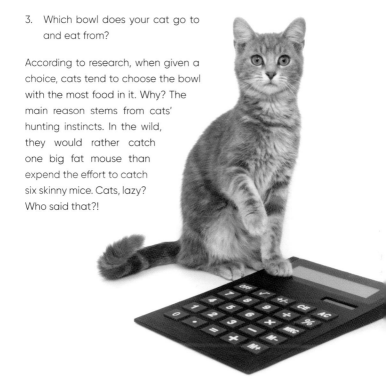

GET
MOVING

Your cat's physical agility is quite amazing. They have incredible balance and flexibility, astonishing reflexes, can jump six times their length and can squeeze through impossibly small gaps. Some people even argue that cats are liquid given their prowess for pouring themselves into the most unlikely of vessels, regardless of their size!

You can take advantage of your cat's cool moves with the brain training games in this section. Combine them with the obstacle course in *Games in the garden* on page 84, and before you know it, you'll be winning TV talent shows.

BRAIN GAME: JUMP IT

Aim of the game: To teach your cat to jump up onto a chair or surface. (It can be a very low surface if your cat is elderly, has trouble with its joints or is a kitten.) And yes, it is ironic to be teaching your cat to jump up when you're so regularly telling them to get down!

1. Call your cat over and show them that you have a treat. Kick the game off by throwing the treat up onto the chair and encouraging your cat to jump up to get it. When they do, reward them with another treat and lots of praise.

2. As you practice step 1, introduce the cue word "jump" as your cat leaps up. They'll start to make the association between the word and the action.

3. What goes up, must come down ... The next is to encourage them to reverse the action. Throw a treat to the floor and tell your cat "down" as they chase the treat.

4. An added bonus is being able to entice your cat to stay on the chair. You can do this by bribing them with treats and gradually increasing the time they're in position.

5. As with many games, once your cat has grasped the concept, you can tell them to "jump" and to get "down" without having to use treats. The cue words and some gentle encouragement should be enough.

BRAIN GAME: JUMPING THROUGH HOOPS

Aim of the game: As it says on the tin, to teach your cat to leap spectacularly through a hoop ... or at least to walk through it. Unlike Jump it, this trick doesn't really have any practical use for you as an owner, but it does stimulate your cat's brain and looks impressive to boot!

1. Start with the hoop low to the ground and use a treat to entice your cat to walk through it. Start small and slow!

2. Gradually increase the height you hold the hoop – don't go too high too soon as it may put your perfectionist cat off. Keep luring, and of course, keep rewarding.

3. Before long, your cat will be showing off its gazelle-like agility, leaping through the hoop without a seductive treat in sight.

BRAIN GAME: WIGGLY WEAVING

Aim of the game: An easy exercise that teaches your cat to weave between obstacles (or your legs if you really want to encourage them to trip you up more than they do already).

1. Line up some suitable obstacles for your cat to maneuver around, leaving plenty of space in between. Using a treat, encourage your cat to weave through the first couple of obstacles and then reward them with a treat. Carry on with the next few obstacles, and praise and reward again.

2. When your cat has got the hang of consistently weaving, you can reduce the bribery and only reward them once they've weaved through the whole course of obstacles.

3. Start to impress your family and friends by showing how your cat can weave through chair legs, table legs, the legs of your whole family … the possibilities are endless.

BRAIN GAME: TUNNEL RUNNING

Aim of the game: To teach your cat to run through a tunnel. Cats love hiding, so you're unlikely to have trouble getting them to go into the tunnel – it's getting them out that might be harder! You can either buy a pop-up tunnel or drape a sheet or blanket to create your own.

1. Encourage your cat into the tunnel by placing some treats in it.

2. Once they're in, get yourself to the other end of the tunnel and entice them out by calling and encouraging. Reward with another treat once they're out.

3. Keep repeating this until your cat is familiar with what you're expecting them to do. Phase out the treats before your cat can't fit through the tunnel!

GAMES
IN THE
GARDEN

Not all cats are the outdoorsy type. If your cat is an indoors/house cat and, for whatever reason, you don't let them outside, you can either adapt the games below or simply keep their indoor environment stimulating with the ideas in the rest of the book. If you have an adventurer who adores exploring the neighbourhood, get set to take your brain training into the Great Outdoors together.

Providing that little bit of extra space, a garden gives your cat plenty of opportunity for vigorous chasing and pouncing. It's a chance to up their energy levels without fear of your best trinkets being sent flying. There are more distractions outside – think butterflies, birds, etc., – so training with your cat might be trickier. Dig deep into your reserves of patience and all will be well.

BRAIN GAME: OBSTACLE COURSE

Aim of the game: To give your cat a great physical workout, at the same time as encouraging them to use their brain to think about how to deal with obstacles. You can do this outside where you have more room, but it can be as much fun inside (although doing it on a slippery floor).

If you don't fancy buying any of the vast range of agility equipment (mainly aimed at dogs) that's available, it's pretty straightforward to create your own obstacles. A garden chair is a perfect jumping obstacle. You can make a tunnel simply by draping a blanket between two objects. Pop a broom handle between two flower pots and you've got a hurdle. Easy! Just make sure it's all safe for your cat.

What are you forgetting? Treats! Of course, you are going to need plenty of treats to hand to coax your cat in the right direction, and to reward them when they complete an activity.

Here are some activities to include that will energise you and your cat (you can refer back to pages 82– 83 for the how to teach the tricks):

- jumping through hoops
- tunnel running
- weaving
- jumping up and over.

Judge your cat's mood. You may find that even if they're super energetic, being led round and round an obstacle course by their human wears thin quite quickly. Keep it at a pace that your cat is happy, with and don't be offended if they wander off. If your cat is older or has physical limitations, you can slow things down and make the obstacles easier. Even a little bit of exercise will help keep them healthier – just don't overdo it.

BRAIN GAME: TREASURE HUNT

Aim of the game: To supercharge your cat's curiosity, fire up their sense of smell and set their natural hunting instinct in motion.

1. Hide some treats outside. To start with, place them in fairly easy-to-find places so your cat knows what's going on and doesn't get frustrated.

2. Give them lots of praise each time they

sniff out a treat. You know your cat's level of praise tolerance, so don't overwhelm them and put them off the hunt.

3. Once your cat gets the idea of the game, you can put the treats in harder-to-find spots. You could even use a hiding spot where your cat has to move something to reach the treat, for example an upturned plastic flower pot.

BRAIN GAME: CLAMBER AND CLIMB

Aim of the game: To stimulate and unleash your cat's natural instinct to climb, even if you've not got a tree in your garden. Cats adore climbing. They like to be up high to survey their kingdom, to keep an eye out for prey and to feel safe and secure.

1. Have a look around your home and garden to find useful components for your homemade cat climbing frame. You can use logs, old branches, offcuts of wood or dismantled wooden furniture (just watch out for any protruding nails) – anything safe for your cat to scale.

2. Start by placing the log, for example, flat on the ground so that your cat has a chance to explore it (and no doubt have a good scratch). If your cat isn't interested at first, entice them on with a treat.

3. As your cat gets accustomed to moving on the log, you can raise it up slightly to give them more of a climbing challenge. Just make sure that the log is secure to prevent any tumbles. The more adventurous your cat gets, the steeper you can make the climb. Just remember to work within your cat's physical ability or they'll get frustrated and lose interest.

HOME
ALONE

We tend to think of cats as being solitary creatures that can be happily left alone. While this is truer for cats than it is for dogs, they do still need human company to make them feel secure – mainly about where the next bowl of food is coming from. Although independent, cats can get bored when left to their own devices for too long. A content cat is far less likely to get up to mischief while you're away.

There are times when you have to leave your cat alone – when you're at work all day, for example. If you've got a kitten under 4 months old, you shouldn't leave them alone for more than 4 hours. The older they get, the more time alone they can cope with. By around 6 months old, they can manage 8 hours by themselves. For adult cats, it really does depend on their temperament. If your cat eats dry food, then with plenty of water and a litter box they can be left safely for 1–2 days, including overnight. But what can you do to keep their brains stimulated in those moments when they're not curled up asleep in your favourite chair?

BRAIN GAME: SCAVENGER HUNT

Aim of the game: To keep your cat's brain busy and their sense of smell entertained with an exciting hunt for treats. (You can also leave favourite toys in hiding places for your cat to discover.)

What could take your cat's mind off being alone more than food?! Create this scavenger hunt by simply hiding dry food or treats around your home. Make sure you hide the food in places your cat is likely to go, for example in the room where their favourite place for sneaking under the bed is. The thrill of the hunt and their tingling nose will keep their brain buzzing and the boredom at bay.

MORE TOP TIPS

- Get your cat a good old-fashioned scratching post.

- Make sure your cat can see out of a window so they can fantasise about chasing birds.

- Leave the TV or radio on to create some soothing sound and a feeling of company.

- Paper bags make an excellent (and cheap) toy to keep your cat busy. Hide some treats or toys inside the bag to give your cat something to hunt out. When the bag is empty, your cat will delight in making it rustle, chasing it and then no doubt ripping it to shreds.

Ensure that any toys you leave out for your cat are safe to be played with unsupervised. So avoid leaving anything with cords that could get caught around your cat's neck, or anything that would be small enough to swallow and potentially cause choking.

THE
CLASSICS

Where would your cat be without some classic tricks in its repertoire? We've already covered some in *Not just for dogs!* (page 90) but there are a few more that any respectable cat should know. The classics are simple, but the wow factor is high. Most importantly, they're easy to do so are perfect for a quick bit of brain training fun whenever you get a spare minute or two with your cat.

BRAIN GAME: SHAKE ON IT

Aim of the game: To teach your cat to shake hands/paws with you. Adorable. Cute. And all other such words. (Remember though that cats aren't overly fond of having their paws touched so they may feel uncomfortable with it at first.)

1. Show your cat that you're holding a treat, then close your fist around it. Presented with a treat they can't reach, your cat will respond by lifting their paw and using it to try to get at it. (Hopefully minus their claws out.)

2. When your cat can do step 1 easily, introduce the cue word "shake". Practice on repeat until your cat has cemented the connection between you putting out a hand and saying the cue. Then is the time to stop using treats. Or maybe just use them occasionally so that your cat doesn't get too disheartened!

NB. Shaking paws can double up as a "high-five" if you're looking to impress a younger generation to whom handshaking is antiquated and for grown-ups only.

BRAIN GAME: DIZZY CAT

Aim of the game: To teach your cat how to spin around like a whirling dervish. Easy to learn but a real show stopper.

1. Hold a treat above your cat's nose. Start to move it in a large circle above their head. Lured by the treat, your cat should follow your hand.

2. Keep your hand (and the treat) rotating. If your cat follows your hand for a whole rotation, give them a stroke and reward them with the treat.

3. If you can get your cat to spin in one full circle, start to add a verbal cue – "spin". This will help your cat make an association in its brain between the command and the action.

4. Providing your cat is happy with the game, slowly increase the number of spins you ask your cat to do before they are rewarded with a treat. Stop before they (or you) get dizzy.

You'll know to stop using treats when your cat can follow your cue word and rotating hand signal. And there you have it – a pirouetting cat.

BRAIN GAME: GIVE US A WAVE

Aim of the game: To teach your cat to wave and melt the heart of anyone within a kilometre radius.

1. This game follows the pattern of *Shake on it* (page 91). When showing your cat the treat, hold it above their nose so that when they try to reach it, they lift up their paw – but don't let them touch your hand as with the Shake on it game. When your cat looks like it's waving, give them a treat!

2. Gradually start to introduce a cue work such as "wave" or "hello". With repeated practice, your cat will learn what to do when they hear the cue word and see you raise your hand. They will be completely unaware of how absolutely irresistible it makes them look.

SOME MORE CLASSICS TO KEEP YOUR CAT BUSY ...

- Pop a couple of treats in an empty cardboard toilet roll and squish each end shut. Give to your cat to play with, and they'll have a ball toying with it and then destroying it to get at the treats.

- Blowing bubbles. Like any toddler worth their salt, cats love chasing bubbles. It gets their brains thinking quickly about how to catch the floating prey. You might enjoy it too!

- Feather on a string on a stick (also known, somewhat mystically, as a cat wand). A great toy for getting your cat moving by encouraging them to jump, pounce and switch on their hunting instinct.

Happy owner, happy cat. Indifferent owner, reclusive cat.

CHINESE PROVERB

DEALING WITH
SPECIFIC
PROBLEMS

ANXIOUS
CATS

Cats are well known for being a little skittish. They are sensitive creatures, which is perhaps why they have a reputation for having a mysterious sixth sense. If you have an anxious cat (see *Be kind, be safe*, page 52, for how to identify anxiety), you may need to go more slowly with them when playing brain games. Perhaps they are a rescue cat that has been mistreated and mistrusts humans, or they could just be naturally timid. Brain game training can be a wonderful way to build their confidence and to encourage them to bond with you – just take a gentler approach so that they don't get frightened.

Remember that behaviour such as hissing could be your cat trying to protect themselves out of fear, not spite. Don't confuse anxiety with aggression. Playing is a great way to release your cat's pent up nervous energy, in the same way that exercise has fantastic benefits for our own mental wellbeing. The more you play with them, the more their confidence will grow.

TIPS FOR TRAINING AN ANXIOUS CAT

- Before doing anything with your cat, make sure they're completely relaxed and comfortable. Stick to familiar environments to increase their sense of security. A stressed cat isn't a willing student.

- Don't overload your cat with too many new things. Take it one step and one brain game at a time. Keep an eye on their body language so that you can tell when their stress levels are rising (see page 96).

- Use lots of treats to help them build those all-important positive associations. A cat that knows what to expect is a happier and more content cat.

- Keep your movements slow – don't startle your cat.

- Keep your own anxiety in check! Or at least try not to show it. Your cat will pick up on any negative signals that you're giving off, which in turn will increase their anxiety levels.

- If your cat is really struggling with engaging and is clearly uncomfortable, take some time out. Stroke them gently to see it that helps. If it doesn't, give your cat some quiet time to themselves so they can calm down.

- A cat pheromone spray can help to create a calming atmosphere, and increase your cat's positive emotions.

BRAIN GAME: IN WITH THE NEW

Aim of the game: To encourage your cat to explore new things and not be afraid of them. Although cats are naturally curious explorers, a nervous cat can find anything that's unfamiliar daunting.

1. When your cat appears to be in a relaxed mood, sit down with them and surround yourselves with a selection of new toys and objects.

2. When your cat approaches an item, reward them with a treat and give lots of praise. Don't play this game for any longer than a few minutes. If your cat appears immediately stressed, simply stop the game before it starts.

3. Next time you play the game, introduce different new objects. Helped along by the treats, your cat will begin to build a positive association with unfamiliar things. This should start to reduce their stress levels when faced with anything they don't know or recognise.

LESS ACTIVE AND
OLDER
CATS

If your cat isn't bursting with the energy of a kitten anymore, how can you ensure they can still benefit from brain training? Perhaps they've got an injury, are currently overweight or old age is starting to slow them down. This doesn't mean that your cat doesn't want to play, nor should you stop playing with them. You can modify many of the games in this book simply by slowing the game down, making it less physical and keeping your play session a little shorter.

When your cat gets older, their brain can deteriorate. Feline cognitive dysfunction syndrome is very similar to Alzheimer's disease in humans. For cats, it can lead to depression, confusion and anti-social behaviour. This is just another reason why play and brain training is so crucial to your cat's wellbeing. By keeping them stimulated, you can help ward against the unfortunate effects of ageing. Brain training certainly isn't a cure-all, but it has marvelous benefits both physically and mentally for your beloved cat.

Many of the brain games in *Not just for dogs!* on page 67 are suitable for less active cats. So try some simple and relatively effort-free things like training your cat to sit or rollover, or to shake paws with you (see page 91). Be mindful of what they can realistically achieve without losing the fun element of brain training. An older cat won't want to initiate play like they once did, so they will need some gentle encouragement.

BRAIN GAME: FIND THE HUMAN

Aim of the game: To spark your cat's hunting instinct without the need for any vigorous expenditure of energy!

1. Rather than hiding food or toys from your cat – hide yourself. Don't worry about feeling silly. You're in your own home, who's going to see you?

2. Either call your cat or wait for them to come looking for you. (Maybe the former in case they decide to take a nap instead.) And don't conceal yourself too well!

3. Be patient if your cat's a little slower these days. They'll love switching into hunting mode to track you down – stimulating all their senses at once.

4. When they find you, reward them generously for their endeavours.

A FEW EXTRAS

Try these other brain stimulating games that are gentle enough for a cat with less bounce:

- Target training – see page 62.

- Any puzzle games that earn your cat treats will make them put their thinking cap on without breaking into a sweat. Try hiding treats under paper cups.

- A plain old piece of crumpled-up paper is sometimes all a cat needs for a bit of gentle chasing and pouncing.

- Encourage your cat to simply follow you around your home (although avoid stairs if, like a Dalek, they find them tricky). This is a really gentle way of encouraging your cat to get physical exercise, and the chance to explore will get their brain ticking.

- Keep games low to the ground. Don't encourage your cat to jump if they're not up to it. If you're not sure, speak to your vet for advice.

- Cat apps – yes, get your cat onto a tablet and into tech! Brain stimulation that only requires a paw to move. See page 116 for more information on how to drag your pet into the 21st century.

HELP!
IT'S NOT
WORKING!

You didn't really think that training your cat was going to be a walk in the park, did you? Your cat's personality – and, of course, yours – will determine your levels of success and how quickly you make progress. As much as it pains to say it again, cats aren't as easy to train as dogs. They're more independent and border on the – some would say – lazy. Plus, they like to believe that they're in charge of us, not vice versa.

That said, stay patient and don't give up – the effort is worth it on all fronts. Here are some of the problems you may encounter, and how you and your cat can overcome them with minimal fuss.

PROBLEM: MY CAT SCRATCHES OR TRIES TO BITE

Fix it: Your cat may have been conditioned to play using its claws. For example, do you scuttle your hand in front of your cat to get a response or encourage them to pounce on your toes as you wiggle them under the duvet? Then you could be partly to blame for pretending to be prey. If you're sure this is just playful behaviour, then remove the temptation for your cat to claw or mouth at you. For example, you can direct your cat's behaviour towards a more appropriate outlet such as a small toy when you're training close to your cat using hand gestures.

If your cat's behaviour is aggressive rather than just misdirected playfulness, consider what is causing the aggression. It may be that a visit to the vet is in order.

PROBLEM: MY CAT ISN'T INTERESTED IN THE SLIGHTEST!

Fix it: Is your cat in the right mindset for play? (See *Encouraging playing*, page 48.) Ensure you're playing together in a quiet, distraction-free place. Remember that cats find other things far more interesting than humans. Are you trying to engage your cat for too long? Experiment with keeping your play sessions shorter, and build them up as your cat becomes more. It could be the game you're playing – if it doesn't float your cat's boat then try something else until you stumble on something that really engages them.

The main thing is to persevere. Trial and error could be the name of the game with your cat. Take it slow and steady, and they will gradually start to appreciate the attention playtime provides them with.

PROBLEM: MY CAT JUST DOESN'T SEEM TO "GET IT"

Fix it: First things first – is it really your cat or is it YOU? Look at what you're doing and how you're behaving. It's vital that you're consistent when you're training your cat – are you sticking to that? If you're not consistent, your cat will simply get confused and have no idea what is expected of them. They'll never learn that way. So, that blank look they're giving you? It's not them being stupid; it's them crying out for you to be consistent and make it easier rather than harder for them.

PROBLEM: NOTHING'S GOING RIGHT AND AND I MIGHT AS WELL GIVE UP!

Fix it: As Peter Gabriel and Kate Bush once sang, "Don't give up, you're not beaten yet". Stay calm and take some deep breaths. Training a pet is hard work and you're doing your best. If you give any sign of stress or frustration when you're with your cat, they cannot fail but to pick up on it. The more stressed you become, the more agitated and resistant to learning your cat will become. Take a break and try again. Tomorrow is another day.

Even if you're not stressed, it could be that your will to make brain training work is overwhelming your cat. Listen to your tone of voice – are you sounding over-excited, too keen? If this isn't the tone your cat knows from their everyday interactions with you, they could be wondering what on earth has happened to you. Concentrate on keeping your tone of voice calm, even, confident and encouraging without verging on desperation!

CAT TAILS

TARA THE HERO

When 4-year-old Jeremy was pulled off his bike by a neighbour's dog and bitten, Tara the family cat was first on the scene. In a daring rescue, Tara leapt at the dog, body slamming it away from Jeremy and chasing it down the driveway. She didn't give up and, with the help of her owner (Jeremy's mum), soon saw the dog off. Jeremy had to have ten stitches in the bite wound.

The video of Tara's heroic actions to save a beloved member of her family has been viewed online more than 5 million times. She's one brave and clever cat.

PWDITAT THE GUIDE CAT

We've all heard of trained guide dogs, but how about a guide cat?

In Wales, Terfel the dog went completely blind due to cataracts. Sadly, Terfel struggled to get about, and eventually became too nervous to try. But then a special cat arrived on the scene. Pwditat was a stray cat taken in by Terfel's owner. The cat and dog rapidly became firm friends, and even slept side by side. Best of all, Pwditat became Terfel's new pair of eyes. Using her paws, Pwditat could guide Terfel around their home, ensuring he didn't bump into walls, and could get outside and enjoy the garden again.

Cats are good masters, as long as you remember what your own place is.

PAUL GRAY

I had been told that the training procedure with cats was difficult. It's not. Mine had me trained in two days.

BILL DANA

TAKING IT TO THE
NEXT
LEVEL

NEXT STEPS:
KEEPING UP THE
MOMENTUM

You've worked your way through the book. Some things have gone brilliantly. Some have gone badly and your cat has turned their back on you and showed you their derrière. Whatever the case, congratulations to both you and your cat! You've made some big steps towards health and happiness. Now's the time to keep up the momentum.

Playing with your cat is about repetition, and your cat loves that – it makes them feel secure. By repeating brain games with your cat, they won't get bored of them (even if you do slightly). Here are some ideas and tips to spice things up a bit if you think it will bolster the benefits:

- Variety is the spice of life. Tempting as it may be to just to play your favourite brain games, don't forget to revisit the games that have proved less successful. Who knows, after a break you might come back to them and find your cat masters the games in a flash. It keeps things challenging if you work on some of the things you've found more difficult rather than just give up on them.

- Up the ante. If you and your cat have got the hang of lots of games, could you up it a level? Providing your cat is physically able, you could make that jump a bit higher, or that weave a bit longer. Use your imagination, but remember not to push your cat too hard or they might lose interest. Even small new challenges are beneficial for stimulating their brain – and yours!

- Get your family involved. While it really needs an adult to train a pet, getting the rest of the family involved is great fun. It's a great way of teaching children how to be responsible for your cat and for animals generally. It's probably best not to get the WHOLE family involved all at once or you risk overwhelming your cat with the attention! You can pass on everything you've learned so that you're not the only brain training expert in the household. It's a good opportunity to find out if you're as good at training your family as you are your cat!

- Invent your own brain games. You're the expert now, so use what you've learnt to dream up some stimulating games of your own. Experience has taught you what your cat does and doesn't like, so make use of that knowledge. If they love hunting around the house, invent a game that focuses on that. You don't need to rely on books like this once you know the basics!

MY CAT
IS A GENIUS!

We all like to think that our own pets are the cleverest in the universe. They are though, aren't they? And we should believe that – it shows we love them. The jury is out on how to measure a cat's cleverness because they are so darned hard to research under lab conditions. But if your cat has mastered all the tricks in this book without a bat of their sleepy eyes, it's a good sign that they've got it all going on up there.

Is it possible to tell whether your cat is actually of above average intelligence? Experts have suggested that the following are good indicators:

- Great communication skills: your cat can meow in different ways for different needs and you can clearly identify what they're trying to tell you.

- Object permanence: they can find an item that has been hidden or moved – i.e. they know that it hasn't just magically vanished into thin air.

- Your cat is able to get along well with people and other animals.

(What is meant by "get along well" isn't clear, but presumably it means no claws or teeth!)

- They are skilled at catching things, whether that be an insect or a feather on a stick. (Try watching a nature programme on TV with your cat. If they watch the "prey" intently, it's a good sign of intelligence, even if they don't initially realise the prey is only a picture.)

Just like with geniuses of the human variety, a clever cat won't excel in all these areas, but they may be an absolute master of one. Every cat has its own individual strengths. Not being able to jump through a hoop doesn't make your cat stupid.

If you are so inclined, there are of course IQ tests your cat can do. (Some even promise a certificate ...). Is it worth IQ testing your cat? Maybe just for fun. It doesn't really mean anything. What is more important is that you know what your cat can do, and that you work with that to keep their brain stimulated. Brain training isn't about showing off how clever your cat is or increasing their intelligence – it's about exercising your cat's brain to keep them mentally healthy and therefore happy.

CAT FACTS
A CAT'S SIXTH SENSE

Cats and many other animals have been revered and feared for an apparent ability to predict events such as storms, earthquakes and other natural disasters. More recently, it's been suggested that cats can detect when humans are ill. Is this coincidence or a mysterious sixth sense lurking deep in your cat's brain?

- Earthquakes are usually always preceded by small tremors that can be detected by specialist equipment. Cats are incredibly sensitive to vibrations, and can detect these tremors through their feet and their whiskers. Rather than a sixth sense, it's more likely that cats pick up these small initial tremors and that's what makes them agitated.

- Volcanoes. Like earthquakes, the imminent eruption of a volcano can be detected through small tremors – again a cat can easily pick up on this. A cat's sensitive sense of smell would also be able to detect the chemicals that a volcano releases into the air before it erupts.

- Storms generate electrical activity that can be detected by your cat's whiskers and fur. Their powerful nose will also sniff out the increase in the ozone in the air as a storm is brewing.

- Human illness is also said to have its own smell and taste. Like dogs, cats can detect this with their super senses. (See *Oscar the Care Home Cat* on page 77.)

It seems that rather than having a sixth sense, your cat's superpowers come from their amazing senses of hearing and smell. As their senses are superior to ours, it's not really all that surprising that they're one step ahead of us.

RECORD BREAKING CATS

- Largest litter: In 1970, a Burmese–Siamese cross gave birth to 19 kittens. The average litter for a domestic cat is 5.

- Longest whiskers: These belonged to Missi, a Maine coon from Finland. Her whiskers measured a whopping 19 cm (7.5 in).

- Oldest cat: Creme Puff, from Texas in the USA, was born in 1967 and died in 2005. 38 years old!

- Loudest purr: The loudest purr by a domestic cat was measured in 2015 and was 67.8 decibels. This extraordinary purr belonged to Merlin from the UK.

- Longest cat: Barivel, a Maine Coon cat from Italy, holds this record. He measures an incredible 120 cm (3 ft 11.2 in).

- Smallest cat: Mr. Peebles, a 2-year-old domestic cat from Illinois, USA, holds the record for the smallest living cat. He weighs just 3 lbs and is 6.1 inches high.

- Most toes: Eighteen toes are the normal number for cats. Jake, from Canada, holds this record with his 27 toes.

- Richest cat: The world's wealthiest cat ever was Blackie. In 1988, he inherited an estate worth $13 million when his owner, a British antiques dealer, died.

CATNOLOGY AND THE
FUTURE

Call it the future or call it cashing in on humans, there's no question that the fast pace of technology is having an impact on our pets' lives. While your cat might not be automated (yet), many of your interactions with them already are.

You can use technology to keep an eye on your cat when you're away from home. Or should that be to allay your guilt when you've left them alone? Set up cameras in your home that connect to an app on your smart phone, and you can check what your cat is up to whenever you want (if you enjoy watching them mainly sleep). You can then use the app to post constant photos to social media and thoroughly bore your friends.

But that's not all:

- Worried that your cat is going to miss out on treats when you're not there? Luckily, you can buy an automatic treat dispenser that can be activated remotely from your phone.

- Possibly TMI (too much information) for some cat owners, but there's a product that you can put under your cat's litter tray to monitor their movements – literally. It records your cat's weight and number of toilet visits, among other "vital" statistics. The idea is that spotting any changes in toilet habits gives an early warning signal of any health issues. Sadly, it doesn't clean out the tray for you.

- Fitbit for your cat? Absolutely. Wearable technology has reached the feline world too. Your cat can wear a collar with a device that measures their temperature, pulse and activity levels. All delivered straight to an app on your phone, of course.

If you're looking for catnology that's going to stimulate your cat's brain rather than your curiosity about their bodily functions, then look no further than app games for cats. There are more available than you can wave a cat wand at. Fishing games, butterfly chasing, pinball, relaxation apps and painting apps – you and your cat will be spoilt for choice. A word for the wise though – there is a real danger of your cat's awesome claws scratching the screen of your tablet or smart phone while playing these games, so stick to an old device that you're not precious about.

CAT FACTS

YOUR CAT'S BRAIN:
THE SCIENCE BIT

- A domesticated cat's brain is about 5cm long and weighs 9 oz.

- The largest brains in the cat family belong to the tigers of Java and Bali (sadly now hunted to extinction).

- The surface area of your cat's cerebral cortex is around 13 square inches. The human brain has a surface area of approximately 388 square inches.

- Your cat's brain structure is 90% similar to a human brain.

- Cats have 300 million neurons in their brain. Dogs have a mere 160 million neurons in comparison, making cats' brains far more complex.

- If you look at the ratio of brain mass to body mass, your cat's brain takes up 0.9% of its total body mass. This compares to human brains that make up about 2% of total body mass, and dogs' brains 1.2%.

- Your cat's brain has 1,000 times more data storage than an iPad!

My cat never laughs or complains, he is always reasoning.

MIGUEL DE UNAMUNO

CAT TAILS
MASHA THE LIFESAVER

Masha was a cat living as a communal pet among the residents of an apartment block in Obninsk, Russia. Russia in January is an extremely cold place, and one day a resident came across Masha tucked up as usual in the box she slept in. However, what was unusual was that Masha was meowing and didn't get up to greet the woman as she normally would do.

The woman was puzzled so went closer to investigate. She was amazed to find a baby in the box with Masha. The baby boy turned out to be around 12 weeks old and had been abandoned. Without Masha keeping him warm, it is extremely unlikely that the baby would have survived.

What's more, Masha tried to get in the ambulance with the baby. A savior to the very last!

OZZIE THE EXPLORER

In 2015, a stray cat turned up in Northern Ireland. When his microchip was scanned, it emerged that he had originally been chipped in Australia, making his journey some 12,000 miles! This plucky cat was named Ozzie by the animal welfare organisation caring for him.

What's more, the microchip also revealed that Ozzie had been born in 1989 – this made him 25 years old. Pretty impressive considering that the average lifespan for a cat is 15 years. Ozzie appeared to be in good health and none the worse for wear for his epic trip.

Quite how Ozzie managed this astonishing journey or how long it took him, no one will ever know. Who knows what adventures he had along the way? Travelling clearly agreed with him, so perhaps we humans should be looking to Ozzie for the secret of a long and happy life!

CAT TAILS
KULI THE SURF DUDE

If you're visiting Honolulu, you might be lucky enough to see a rare sight – a cat surfing. Kuli, who also only has one eye, has been surfing with his owners since he was 6 months old. He was found severely malnourished and, after surgery to remove his infected eye, was lovingly nursed back to health – including lots of baths, which helped develop his love of water.

Kuli was slowly introduced to beach life and taught to swim wearing a cat-sized life jacket. He now rides the waves on the front of his owners' board or on their shoulders, loving every minute of it.

Unsurprisingly, Kuli became an online sensation after videos of his daredevil antics were published. And, of course, he now has his own Instagram account with over 56,000 followers!

TAMA THE
STATIONMASTER
(AND GODDESS)

Kishi train station in Japan had a most unusual stationmaster. Tama the cat was officially appointed into the role in 2007, and is credited with turning around the fortunes of the near-bankrupt station.

Wearing a custom-made stationmaster's cap, Tama would position herself at the ticket gate to survey the passengers arriving and leaving. Her story soon spread and she became famous, attracting tourists from all over Japan. During her 8-year occupancy, Tama is said to have boosted the local economy by over £5 million, simply by the number of visitors she attracted to the area.

Sadly, Tama died in 2015. At her funeral, she was elevated to the status of goddess as part of the Shinto religion, the religion practiced by many Japanese.

BRAIN TRAINING
NOTES

Use this space below to make a note of the brain games you've tried with your cat. You can jot down what went well (and what went badly!), things to try slightly differently next time and any observations on what your cat did and didn't like. Try to revisit and add to your notes regularly to see how you and your cat have progressed. Good luck!